BUTTERFLIES

BUTTERFLIES

By Ruth Tepper Brown

INCREDI
BUILDS

A Division of Insight Editions, LP
San Rafael, California

JEWELS IN FLIGHT

Do you know someone who's a social butterfly? It means they flit from group to group with ease.

Have you ever heard of the butterfly effect? It's what scientists call the possibility that even a tiny change in one place (like the air disturbed by the flap of a butterfly's wing) can result in a big change in another (like a tornado).

Colorful, elegant, and seemingly carefree, the butterfly has found its way into many parts of our lives. You may know someone who's dressed up as a butterfly, tried an arm-swirling butterfly stroke in a swimming pool, or seen *Madame Butterfly* at the opera (it's a story about lost love).

BUT WHAT ABOUT REAL BUTTERFLIES? Have you seen one lately? If so, count yourself lucky. A butterfly's life is short and fraught with danger. These delicate insects spend most of their lives as eggs, and then caterpillars, before transforming into the elegant creatures that grace our gardens—sometimes only for a few, brief days.

In fact, the flitting, fluttering butterfly is only one small part of this amazing creature's life story.

Along with moths, butterflies belong to an order of flying insects called lepidoptera, a word that means "scaled wings." Of the more than 200,000 lepidoptera species, only about ten percent—20,000—are butterflies.

BUTTERFLY WORLD

Butterflies live all over the world—wherever there are plants for caterpillars to eat and flowers for butterflies to sip from. Keep an eye out, and you may be able to spot the butterflies that live near you.

BUTTERFLIES OF NORTH AMERICA

WESTERN TIGER SWALLOWTAIL
Papilio rutulus

ORANGE MONARCH
Danaus plexippus

BLOMFILD'S BEAUTY
Smyrna blomfildia

EASTERN TIGER SWALLOWTAIL
Papilio glaucus

PAINTED LADY
Vanessa cardui

GLASSWINGED BUTTERFLY
Greta oto

BUTTERFLIES OF SOUTH AMERICA

BLUE MORPHO
Morpho didius

SULKOWSKY'S MORPHO
Morpho Sulkowsky

AMAZON BEAUTY
Baeotus aeilus

STAR SAPPHIRE BUTTERFLY
Asterope sapphire

Butterflies of Australia

MOUNTAIN SWALLOWTAIL

Papilio ulysses

CAIRNS BIRDWING

Ornithoptera euphorion

YELLOW-SPOTTED JEZEBEL

Delias nysa

COMMON BLUEBOTTLE

Graphium sarpedon

Butterflies of Asia

EMERALD SWALLOWTAIL

Papilio palinurus

OLD WORLD SWALLOWTAIL

Papilio machaon

EUROPEAN PEACOCK BUTTERFLY

Aglais io

LIME BUTTERFLY

Papilio demoleus

Butterflies of Africa

COMMON BRIMSTONE

Gonepteryx rhamni

BLUE MOON BUTTERFLY

Hypolimnas bolina

BLOOD RED GLIDER

Cymothoe sangaris

GIANT AFRICAN SWALLOWTAIL

Papilio antimachus

Butterflies of Europe

MOUNTAIN APOLLO

Parnassius apollo

BLACK-VEINED WHITE

Aporia crataegi

MEADOW ARGUS

Junonia villida

BUILT LIKE A BUTERFLY

Like all insects, butterflies have three main body sections, six legs, and a protective exoskeleton. If you've ever noticed a butterfly sitting in the sun, warming itself, that's because insects are cold-blooded. A butterfly can't fly if it gets too cold.

(A) ANTENNAE

A butterfly uses its two antennae (sometimes called "feelers") for both smell and balance.

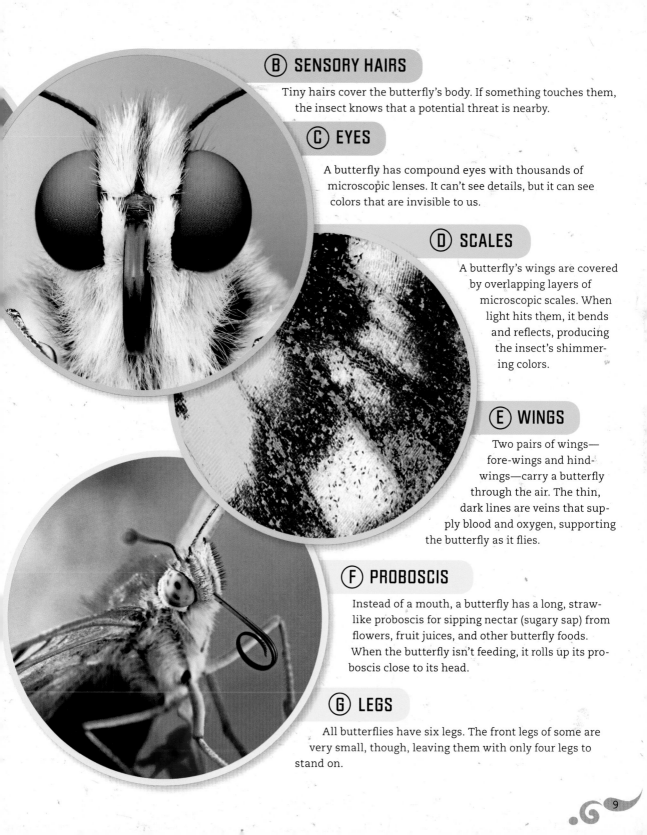

B SENSORY HAIRS

Tiny hairs cover the butterfly's body. If something touches them, the insect knows that a potential threat is nearby.

C EYES

A butterfly has compound eyes with thousands of microscopic lenses. It can't see details, but it can see colors that are invisible to us.

D SCALES

A butterfly's wings are covered by overlapping layers of microscopic scales. When light hits them, it bends and reflects, producing the insect's shimmering colors.

E WINGS

Two pairs of wings—fore-wings and hind-wings—carry a butterfly through the air. The thin, dark lines are veins that supply blood and oxygen, supporting the butterfly as it flies.

F PROBOSCIS

Instead of a mouth, a butterfly has a long, straw-like proboscis for sipping nectar (sugary sap) from flowers, fruit juices, and other butterfly foods. When the butterfly isn't feeding, it rolls up its proboscis close to its head.

G LEGS

All butterflies have six legs. The front legs of some are very small, though, leaving them with only four legs to stand on.

BUTTERFLY LIFE CYCLE

Butterflies reproduce by laying eggs. But when an egg hatches, it's not a baby butterfly that flits out. Instead, a tiny caterpillar is born. Over time, the caterpillar goes through a series of changes called metamorphosis (me-ta-MOR-fa-sis)—one of nature's most amazing transformations—and an adult butterfly emerges.

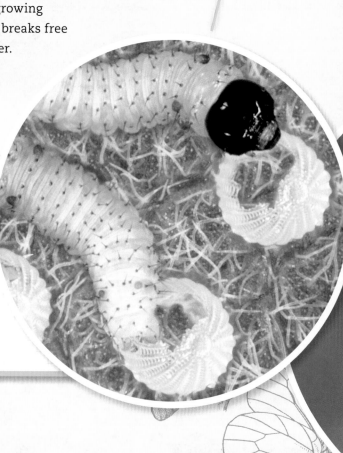

METAMORPHOSIS OF A MONARCH
(Danaus Plexippus)

It takes four or five days for a monarch butterfly egg to hatch. When the caterpillar emerges, it spends about two weeks eating and growing before forming a chrysalis. The adult breaks free from the chrysalis about ten days later.

1. EGG

Female monarch butterflies lay tiny, pinhead-sized eggs on milkweed—the only plants the caterpillars will eat. The closer the eggs get to hatching, the more transparent they become. You can see the tiny caterpillars inside.

2. CATERPILLAR (LARVA)

All of the butterfly's growth happens in this stage, so the caterpillar's main job is to eat and grow. When it gets too big for its skin, the caterpillar wiggles out, and a new layer of skin forms around it. This process is called molting. Caterpillars molt several times as they grow but retain their soft, flexible bodies.

3. CHRYSALIS (PUPA)

When the caterpillar has finished growing, it attaches itself to a stem or leaf and, hanging upside down, forms a chrysalis. On the outside, the chrysalis doesn't move. But inside, it's transforming into a butterfly. Just before the adult emerges, its color develops, and you can see the new butterfly through the thinning chrysalis.

4. ADULT

The butterfly emerges from its chrysalis with wrinkled wings folded against its body. It pumps blood into its wings to expand them and, after about an hour, flies off to find food. The main job of the adult butterfly is to reproduce. Most monarch butterflies will only live five or six weeks, but the females will lay up to seven hundred eggs in that time span, beginning the process all over again.

FINDING FOOD

When a butterfly lays her eggs, she needs to be sure there's food nearby to feed the soon-to-be-born caterpillars. Many will eat just one specific pant, called a "host" plant, so she's careful to find just the right spot.

Rather than laying her eggs all in one place, a butterfly may lay small broods on several different host plants to give the newborns the best chance of survival. Birds, bats, frogs, spiders, beetles—pretty much any insect-eating animal—are happy to find caterpillars to eat, so only a few from each group of eggs may survive.

A caterpillar's mouth is perfect for ripping, chewing, and swallowing. The caterpillar grabs onto a leaf or stem with its front legs and uses the jagged edges of its jaws to tear into its food. (When gardeners start to notice their dying plants looking like lace, they know to look for a caterpillar nearby!)

As it eats, the caterpillar grows and molts several times before it reaches full size—which may be thousands of times bigger than it began. Only when it's done growing will it transform into an adult butterfly.

As soon as the adult emerges from its chrysalis and is ready to fly, it heads out to look for something to eat. Unlike its larval (caterpillar) stage, the adult butterfly no longer has a mouth and jaws to eat with. Instead, it has a tube-like proboscis that works more like a straw. Now, rather than eating leaves and stems, the adult can only dine on liquids.

Most butterflies drink sugar-rich nectar, a sticky liquid produced by flowers. Many also sip juice from fallen fruit or feed on tree sap. A few kinds of butterflies, including the harveser (Feniseca tarquinius) and the male purple emperor (Apatura iris), are meat-eaters, sucking up fluids from decaying animals.

Purple emperor

ON THE MOVE

Butterflies are cold-blooded, so those that live in colder climates need to survive through freezing winter temperatures. Most wait out the winter as caterpillars or chrysalises. But some, like the monarch, migrate to warmer climates, as birds do.

In the fall, monarchs from the eastern half of the United States and Canada travel down through Texas to spend the winter in Mexico.

Western monarchs migrate out to the Pacific coast. There, they gather in and around the town of Pacific Grove, California, returning to the same trees they come to every year. Tens of thousands may gather on a single tree, clumping together to keep warm. Scientists aren't sure how they know to go to those trees or why they gather there in the first place, since they're never the same butterflies that were there before.

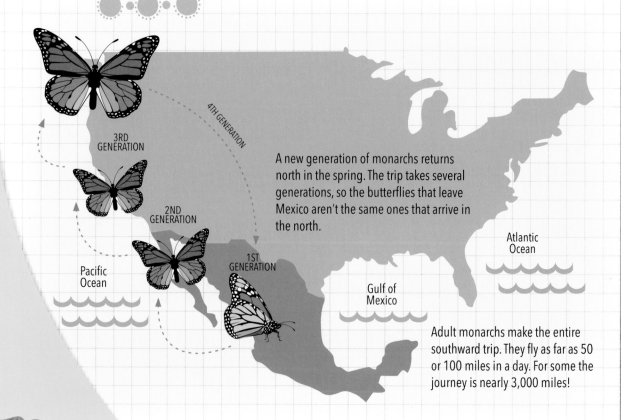

4TH GENERATION

3RD GENERATION

2ND GENERATION

1ST GENERATION

Pacific Ocean

A new generation of monarchs returns north in the spring. The trip takes several generations, so the butterflies that leave Mexico aren't the same ones that arrive in the north.

Atlantic Ocean

Gulf of Mexico

Adult monarchs make the entire southward trip. They fly as far as 50 or 100 miles in a day. For some the journey is nearly 3,000 miles!

Monarch butterflies are the only ones known to make two-way journeys, but other kinds of butterflies will move north when the weather begins to warm or south when it starts to get cold. Even in places where it's warm all the time, butterflies may migrate away from their home territories to start new colonies, especially if they need to find new food sources.

Monarch butterflies

BUTTERFLY OR MOTH?

Butterflies and moths are closely related. They both start out as caterpillars and change into their adult forms. They eat the same kinds of foods, look similar, and lay eggs, but there are some telltale differences. How can you tell them apart? Sometimes, scientists have to delve deeper, looking at things like wing attachments and internal organs to figure it out. Can you tell the butterfly from the moth?

WHAT TIME OF DAY IS IT?

If it's daytime, it's probably a butterfly. Butterflies are diurnal—awake in the daytime. If it's night-time, it's probably a moth. Moths are nocturnal—active at night.

BUTTERFLY

WHAT DO ITS ANTENNAE LOOK LIKE?

Most butterflies have club-tipped or hooked antennas. Moths more often have feathery antennae or antennae with jagged edges. Both use their antennas to sense chemicals in the air that give them information about smell, including when a potential mate is nearby.

WHAT'S IT DOING WITH ITS WINGS?

If the resting insect holds its wings out flat or folds them onto its back, it's probably a moth. A butterfly is more likely to rest with its wings held together straight up above its body.

The colorful flier here is a garden tiger moth (*Arctia caja*). It may look like a butterfly, but it's actually a moth, even though it flies around during the day. (Check out its fuzzy antennas.)

HOW BIG IS IT?

Moths are usually (but not always) smaller than butterflies.

HOW FAT IS IT?

Most butterflies have thinner bodies than moths. The fatter its abdomen, the more likely it is to be a moth.

WHAT COLOR IS IT?

As a rule, butterflies are generally more colorful than moths, but there are some brightly colored moths and dull-colored butterflies as well.

WHAT DOES ITS PUPA LOOK LIKE?

If you find a bare pupa attached to a branch or leaf, it's a developing butterfly in a chrysalis. Moths develop in cocoons—pupas encased in silk.

The fat-bodied, dull-looking insect, on the other hand, is a Juvenal's Duskywing (*Erynnis juvenalis*)–a butterfly. It has hooked antennas but rests with its wings open flat.

HOW NOT TO BE EATEN

At every stage in a butterfly's development—egg, caterpillar, adult—there is some animal happy to make it a meal. Ants and beetles eat butterfly eggs. Birds, bats, frogs, spiders, lizards, and even monkeys are fond of eating caterpillars and butterflies. But the insects do have a few ways to evade capture.

Giant swallowtail caterpillar

FLUTTER BY

A butterfly's fluttery, twisty flight pattern makes it hard for predators to catch. Rather than flapping like birds, butterflies beat their wings in a figure-eight pattern, which makes them rise and fall unpredictably. Poisonous butterflies fly more directly, knowing they won't be bothered by predators who recognize them.

BLEND IN

Caterpillars and butterflies that look like other things around them use camouflage to hide in plain sight. The Indian leaf butterfly (*Kallima inachus*) looks like a dried up leaf, so predators don't notice it. The giant swallowtail caterpillar (*Papilio cresphontes*) looks like a bird dropping.

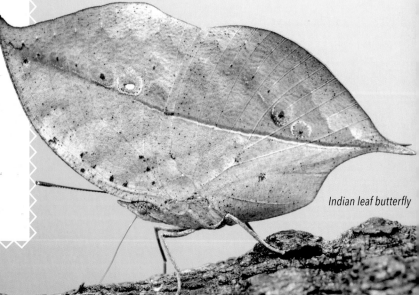

Indian leaf butterfly

TASTE BAD
(OR LOOK LIKE SOMETHING THAT TASTES BAD)

The pipevine swallowtail (*Battus philenor*) tastes bad and makes birds sick, so they avoid eating it. The spicebush swallowtail (*Papilio troilus*) doesn't taste bad (to a bird, anyway), but it looks like a pipevine swallowtail, so birds avoid it, too. Bad-tasting butterflies are often the most brightly colored, so birds will recognize them— and stay away.

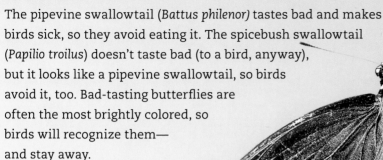

Pipevine swallowtail

Peacock butterfly

LOOK SCARY

Some butterflies have big "eye-spots" on their wings to make predators think they're looking at a bigger, scarier animal. Eyespots on the peacock butterfly (*Aglais io*), for instance, can make a predator wonder what it's looking at.

BECOME AN ESCAPE ARTIST

The layers of scales on a butterfly's wing can actually help it escape from spider webs. Scales that get caught in a web can detach, helping the butterfly make its escape.

THE RECORD HOLDERS

Scientists find new kinds of butterflies all the time, so record holders come and go, but here are a few noteworthy specimens.

BIGGEST

The biggest known butterfly is the female Queen Alexandra's birdwing (*Ornithoptera alexandrae*). With a wingspan of 11 inches (28 cm), it's as wide as a dinner plate.

Grizzled skipper

SMALLEST

The smallest known butterflies are the eastern and western pygmy blues (*Brephidium isophthalma* and *Brephidium exilis*, respectively). They have wingspans of just half an inch (1.25 cm), which is smaller than a dime.

Blue pygmy

FASTEST

Skipper butterflies can fly faster than 30 miles per hour (48 kph).

RAREST

Several kinds of butterflies are thought to be very rare and in danger of extinction. The last group of St. Francis' satyr (*Neonympha mitchellii francisci*), for instance, is found only on a military base in North Carolina. The Palos Verdes blue (*Glaucopsyche lygdamus palosverdesensis*) was thought extinct until a small population was rediscovered near a fuel storage facility in Los Angeles.

St. Francis' satyr

MOST COMMON

The cabbage white (*Pieris rapae*) is thought to be the most common butterfly on the planet. The caterpillar is considered a pest, since it likes to dine on farmers' cabbages and kale.

Cabbage white

SLOWEST

Some butterflies, including the Little Wood Satyr (*Megisto cymela*), are slow fliers, sometimes moving at just 5 miles per hour (8 kph).

Little wood satyr

WHY BUTTERFLIES MATTER

Butterflies are one of nature's most elegant creatures, and for centuries people have celebrated their beauty and charm. The sight of a butterfly is heartwarming and spiritually uplifting—but butterflies are also important for science and the environment.

Because butterflies have such short lives, scientists can study many generations to understand how they pass on their genes and how that affects the way we all grow and live. The amazing way butterflies navigate—especially migrating monarchs—is also something scientists are trying to understand.

In the wild, butterflies flit from flower to flower helping to pollinate plants, including the fruits and vegetables we rely on for food. Around the world, scientists and butterfly watchers count the number of butterflies and caterpillars they see each year. They know that having butterflies around is a sign of a healthy environment. And strange as it may seem, the fact that butterflies and caterpillars are food sources for other animals is an important part of the balance of nature, too.

Each year, several butterfly species either become extinct, disappearing from the earth forever, or face extinction. Whenever people cut down the trees that butterflies need for food, it puts these delicate creatures at risk.

Nobody is quite sure where the word "butterfly" comes from, but it began in Old English as buttorfleoge (but-tor-FLOO-ga). Some think yellow butterflies simply reminded people of the color of butter. Others think the word described flying insects common in the spring, when butter was traditionally made.

GROW A BUTTERFLY GARDEN!

It's a rare treat to see a beautiful butterfly. But there are things you can do to see them more often—or even encourage them to live nearby.

Whether you live in a city or on a farm, you can attract butterflies by offering food and shelter. A slice of fruit in a saucer of water and some flowering plants set outside in pots is all you need to begin.

If you have more space, consider planting the brightly colored flowers that butterflies prefer. Flowers like marigolds, cosmos, nasturtium, and lavender are easy to grow, can create a beautiful space, and give butterflies access to the sweet nectar they need to survive. Some people even build leaf-filled "butterfly boxes" to help butterflies survive cold weather. Plants like hollyhock, goldenrod, and oregano can keep caterpillars happy, too.

If you're lucky, you'll be able to find a chrysalis to watch and see a butterfly emerge.

PLACES TO VISIT

Some cities have zoos and botanical gardens with butterfly houses—greenhouses where all sorts of live butterflies are on display to the public. If there's one in your area, check it out. You'll be able to see some of the most beautiful butterflies in the world. Some museums also have natural history displays showing hundreds of butterflies that have been collected by scientists for study.

MAKE IT YOUR OWN

One of the great things about IncrediBuilds™ models is that each one is completely customizable. The untreated, natural wood can be decorated with paints, pencils, pens, beads, sequins—the list goes on and on!

BEFORE YOU BEGIN

Before you start building and decorating your model, read through the included instruction sheet so you understand how all the pieces come together. Then make a plan–polka dots, diamonds, or just doodles? What about a ballerina butterfly? The choice is yours! Here are some sample projects to get those creative juices flowing.

The butterfly model is almost always easier to paint fully assembled. If you want to paint the wings separate, though, make sure you use a very thin coat of paint so the wings will still fit on the model.

MONARCH BUTTERFLY

The outline of the wood model you've built is actually fashioned after a swallowtail butterfly. But that shouldn't stop you from being creative. You can turn your model into any butterfly you like with a little imagination. Here's an example of the iconic migrating monarch.

 1 Start by painting the body and the antennae of the model black.

 2 Next, paint the wings orange. Let dry.

 3 Go back and outline the wings in black as shown in the photo. Let dry.

 4 To finish, use a toothpick to add white dots to the black sections.

WHAT YOU NEED:
- Paintbrush
- Orange, black, and white paint
- Toothpick

SEQUINS IN SPRING

You can use just about any art supply to decorate your model. Try sequins on this spring-themed butterfly.

WHAT YOU NEED:

- Paintbrush
- Brown, black, and light blue paint
- Toothpick

WHAT YOU MIGHT WANT:

- Tweezers

1 Start by painting the body and antennae of the model. The sample shows a brown body with black antennae.

2 Paint the wings light blue. Let dry.

3 Place a small dot of glue on the bottom of the sequin and lay it onto the wings. Keep adding sequins until you get the effect you like.

GLITTER GALORE!

A butterfly's wings may glitter in the sunlight, so why can't your model?

For this project, paint and glitter the wings while they're separate from the body of the model.

WHAT YOU NEED:

- Paintbrush
- Paint in any color you like
- Toothpick
- Decoupage glue
- Sequins

WHAT YOU MIGHT WANT:

- Glitter glue
- Foam paintbrush

TIP

If you want to save the glitter, shake the excess onto a piece of blank paper and funnel it back into the bottle.

1. Paint the body and antennae of the butterfly. A pink body and yellow antennae were used for the sample, but any color combination you like will work. You can use black paint or pen to fill in the eyes.

2. Paint the wings a solid color. Orange is used here. Let dry.

3. Brush a thin layer of glue on one wing.

4. Shake glitter over the glue and let set. Then shake the excess glitter off.

5. Repeat steps 3 and 4 with all four wings. Let dry.

6. Attach the wings to the model to finish.

For the body, you can add glitter the way you did for the wings, or try some glitter glue for extra sparkle!

STEAMPUNK

There are many ways to describe Steampunk style. It's essentially a vintage style with a steam-powered science-fiction twist. You can play with it to find the version you like best, but here's a version of a mechanical-looking butterfly to get you started.

WHAT YOU NEED:

- Paintbrush
- Gold, bronze, and black paint
- Decoupage glue
- Found objects (Look at your local craft store for jewelry or scrapbooking embellishments you can use. Gears, clock hands, and even keys are ideal.)

1 Start by painting the body of the model bronze.

2 Paint the interior section of the wings bronze.

3 Paint the outside of the wings gold.

4 Use black paint to add details as you like. Here black paint was used to make the change from gold to bronze.

5 Add a drop of glue where you want your embellishments. Press your embellishment onto the glue carefully and let dry.

6 Keep adding embellishments until you are happy with your creation!

31

IncrediBuilds™
A Division of Insight Editions, LP
PO Box 3088
San Rafael, CA 94912
www.incredibuilds.com
www.insighteditions.com

Find us on Facebook: www.facebook.com/InsightEditions

Follow us on Twitter: @insighteditions

Library of Congress Cataloging-in-Publication Data available.

ISBN: 978-1-68298-007-1

Publisher: Raoul Goff
Associate Publisher, Children's Division: Jon Goodspeed
Art Director: Chrissy Kwasnik
Designer: Ashley Quackenbush
Project Editor: Rebekah Piatte
Managing Editor: Alan Kaplan
Production Editors: Lauren LePera and Carly Chillmon
Editorial Assistants: Erum Khan and Holly Fisher
Associate Production Manager: Sam Taylor
Model Designer: Cuiling Ke, TeamGreen

ROOTS of PEACE   REPLANTED PAPER

Insight Editions, in association with Roots of Peace, will plant two trees for each tree used in the manufacturing of this book. Roots of Peace is an internationally renowned humanitarian organization dedicated to eradicating land mines worldwide and converting war-torn lands into productive farms and wildlife habitats. Roots of Peace will plant two million fruit and nut trees in Afghanistan and provide farmers there with the skills and support necessary for sustainable land use.

MANUFACTURED IN CHINA

10 9 8 7 6 5 4 3 2 1

Image Credits

Page 1: Mirek Kijewski/shutterstock.com

Page 2: ANATOL/shutterstock.com (bottom left); Peter Waters/shutterstock.com (top left); Marco Uliana/shutterstock.com (bottom right); Peter Waters/shutterstock.com (top right)

Page 3: Mirek Kijewski/shutterstock.com (top); Vitolga/shutterstock.com (bottom left); MarkMirror/shutterstock.com (bottom right)

Page 4: anekoho/shutterstock.com

Page 5: Butterfly Hunter/shutterstock.com

Page 6: From left to right: alslutsky/shutterstock.com; Christian Musat/shutterstock.com; Vitolga/shutterstock.com; Leighton Photography & Imaging/shutterstock.com; paulrommer/shutterstock.com; Peter Waters/shutterstock.com; ANATOL/shutterstock.com; ANATOL/shutterstock.com; Marco Uliana/shutterstock.com; Marco Uliana/shutterstock.com

Page 7: From left to right: Hanka Steidle/shutterstock.com; nexus 7/shutterstock.com; Peter Waters/shutterstock.com; Super Prin/shutterstock.com; Sailorr/shutterstock.com; Mirek Kijewski/shutterstock.com; MarkMirror/shutterstock.com; BOONCHUAY PROMJIAM/shutterstock.com; Vitalii Hulai/shutterstock.com; lapetitelumiere/shutterstock.com; Marco Uliana/shutterstock.com; RichardCH/shutterstock.com; Marco Uliana/shutterstock.com; Christian Musat / shutterstock.com; MarkMirror/shutterstock.com

Page 8: Cbenjasuwan/shutterstock.com (bottom); Ireneusz Waledzik/shutterstock.com (top right)

Page 9: Jakub Zak/shutterstock.com (top); wanchai/shutterstock.com (middle); Stephen Pire/shutterstock.com (bottom)

Page 10: Cathy Keifer/shutterstock.com

Page 11: Thomas Morris/shutterstock.com (top); del.Monaco/shutterstock.com (bottom)

Page 12: Roylee_photosunday/shutterstock.com (top); Cornel Constantin/shutterstock.com (bottom)

Page 13: Sari ONeal/shutterstock.com (top); MarkMirror/shutterstock.com (bottom)

Page 15: Michael Warwick/shutterstock.com (top); Yuval Helfman/shutterstock.com (bottom)

Page 16: Jim and Lynne Weber/shutterstock.com (right); Johan Larson/shutterstock.com (left)

Page 17: Damian Money/shutterstock.com (top left); Hway Kiong Lim/shutterstock.com (bottom left); undefined/shutterstock.com (top right); THEJAB/shutterstock.com (bottom right)

Page 18: Marco Uliana/shutterstock.com (top right); Tyler Fox/shutterstock.com (top left); twospeeds/shutterstock.com (bottom)

Page 19: Phase4Studios/shutterstock.com (top); MarkMirror/shutterstock.com (middle); Nikola Rahme/shutterstock.com (bottom)

Page 20: rybalov77/shutterstock.com (top); Forest man72/shutterstock.com (bottom left); Reddogs/shutterstock.com (bottom right)

Page 21: Gerald A. DeBoer/shutterstock.com (top); Brian Lasenby/shutterstock.com (bottom); cliff collings/shutterstock.com (middle)

Page 22: Vojta Kulhanek/shutterstock.com

Page 23: Beata Becla/shutterstock.com (top); Blend Images/shutterstock.com (bottom)

Page 24: Martha Marks/shutterstock.com

Page 25: gali estrange/shutterstock.com